ᵀᴴᴱBOSTON
FREEDOM TRAIL®

THE BOSTON
FREEDOM TRAIL®
In WORDS *and* PICTURES

ROBERT WHEELER

Photography by Anna Solo • Foreword by Jim Koch • Preface by Dan McCole

Skyhorse Publishing

Skyhorse Publishing books may be purchased in bulk at special discounts for sales promotion, corporate gifts, fund-raising, or educational purposes. Special editions can also be created to specifications. For details, contact the Special Sales Department, Skyhorse Publishing, 307 West 36th Street, 11th Floor, New York, NY 10018 or info@skyhorsepublishing.com.

Skyhorse® and Skyhorse Publishing® are registered trademarks of Skyhorse Publishing, Inc.®, a Delaware corporation.

Visit our website at www.skyhorsepublishing.com.

10 9 8 7 6 5 4 3 2 1

Library of Congress Cataloging-in-Publication Data

Names: Wheeler, Robert, 1963– author. | Solo, Anna, photographer.
Title: The Boston Freedom Trail in words and pictures / Robert Wheeler ; photography
    by Anna Solo ; foreword by Jim Koch ; preface by Dan McCole.
Description: New York City : Skyhorse Publishing, [2019]
Identifiers: LCCN 2018056827 | ISBN 9781510743779 (pbk. : alk. paper)
Subjects: LCSH: Freedom Trail (Boston, Mass.) | Freedom Trail (Boston, Mass.)—Pictorial works. |
    Boston (Mass.)—Pictorial works.
Classification: LCC F73.37 .W54 2019 | DDC 974.4/61—dc23
LC record available at https://lccn.loc.gov/2018056827

Cover design by Qualcom
Cover photograph by Anna Solo

Print ISBN: 978-1-5107-4377-9
Ebook ISBN: 978-1-5107-4378-6

Printed in China

Lovingly dedicated to Emma and Helen.

"Educate your children to the habit of holding passion and an upright and reasoning will, and you have done much to abolish misery from their future."
—Benjamin Franklin

FOREWORD

By Jim Koch, founder of the Boston Beer Company
and brewer of Samuel Adams Boston Lager

When you live in Boston, as I have since 1967, it's easy to take The Freedom Trail for granted. It's even easy to curse its small, circuitous streets and cobblestone paths. Locals often overlook the red brick line that guides curious visitors through the city. But as Bostonians, we all have our moments when we stop and pause in awe of the history that surrounds us.

I had one of those moments of awe when I was starting The Boston Beer Company and was searching for a name for my signature brew. Friends had given me sheaves of possible names when I recalled my high school history teacher's favorite figure from the American Revolution, Samuel Adams. I clearly remembered why I became captivated with Adams: it was his unyielding fervor and his unwavering drive for independence; it was his progressive thinking and his determination to stay in the fight, even against overwhelming odds. For me, his name is synonymous with American pride and independence and freedom. And like me, Samuel Adams came from a family of brewers. I will always remember that spring morning when I gathered my courage and forced myself to take the elevator to the lobby, to walk down State Street, and to make my first terrifying sales call to introduce Samuel Adams Boston Lager.

If Boston is, as Oliver Wendell Holmes claimed in 1858, the "Hub of the Universe," then Faneuil Hall is the hub of Samuel Adams' life. I hope that both Bostonians and visitors alike who walk the Freedom Trail will enjoy this beautifully written book. I am honored that Robert Wheeler asked me to write this foreword. I feel that when reading these expressive paragraphs, and when gazing upon these evocative photographs, one will never again overlook the grand significance of historic Boston and its awe-inspiring Freedom Trail.

Cheers!
Jim Koch

PREFACE

By Dan McCole, Southie Watercolorist

As an Irish American having grown up in South Boston, I have much pride in the major role Boston, my *City on the Hill*, played in the fight for freedom from the British Crown. As a graduate of Boston's Vesper George School of Art in 1952, I have spent a good part of my life painting those images of the city—its people, its architecture, its harbor, its traditions and celebrations—that inspire and resonate.

Through his new book, Robert Wheeler breaks with tradition by bringing to life the bravery, the hopes, the risks, and the edgy promise of a new country for a people who bet their lives on a free society. The words and images within this important book are based on his passion, and his keen observation, as he takes us behind and underneath the physical beauty of the bronze plaques, sculptures, and burial grounds, and fleshes out the lives of a people who were willing to die in order to live free.

As I step along with my life, moving into those more graceful and contemplative years, I am reminded that lasting art reaches into the heart of the observer, thereby keeping images and events fresh and alive. Boston's rich and charismatic Trail, as seen through these lyrical vignettes and these moving pictures, keeps the torch lit, and reminds us of the precious cost, and the beauty, of true and lasting freedom.

Best and Always,
Dan McCole

INTRODUCTION

The beauty and allure of Boston's Freedom Trail—a trail that winds itself through modern buildings, busy traffic, and hurried people—is endlessly captivating, forever surprising, and worthy of contemplation and celebration. There is simply no other city in America that exposes and reflects as much history, and it is the enduring presence of Boston's historical past that makes it an essential destination. This city's past, and that of the entire American experience, can be discovered on each corner and contains fascinating stories of both unanimity and rebellion in the lives of real people struggling to find liberation and dignity in the New World. Those who established a Republic and who envisioned a future governed by and for the people in those early years of the 1770s, were following the philosophy and spirit of the Age of Enlightenment, or Reason, that had first been conceived on the European continent by such writers as Locke, Hume, and Voltaire. These men during this Age believed in, and advanced through a rational and scientific approach, the ideals of liberty, of a constitutional government, and of the separation of church and state. The commitment to the ideals of Enlightenment can be seen in the founding documents of the new Republic, and in the great halls where the ideas of the Revolution were first debated and declared. Boston's Freedom Trail is a constant reminder of the perils of confronting the powerful and, throughout its many twists and turns, one is constantly reminded of the predominance and tyranny of the British monarchy. Due to the power of King George III and his determination to subdue his American colony, colonial rebels—our Founding Fathers—were considered malicious and often referred to as extremists, even terrorists. Those men—Paine, Adams, Jefferson, Hancock, Franklin, Revere—backed by strong and resourceful women, were subject to being hanged for their treasonous denunciations. As a group of thinkers with very radical ideas about liberty, the odds of creating a successful American Revolution, and bringing to power a Constitution based on progressive thinking, were long indeed. But with courage, perseverance, intelligence, and at times simple luck, these undaunted men succeeded in uniting and transforming the country, and later, the world. In addition to its tribute to official historic sites relating to the American Revolution and independence, this famous trail includes other memorials to resistance against world oppression and for liberation, and to America's own post-1783 struggles with freedom and dignity. For example, one will encounter the Shaw Memorial on Boston Common—just steps away from the Black Heritage Trail that winds its way through the living history of Beacon Hill—and one will come upon the Holocaust Memorial near Faneuil Hall. This trail is everlasting, absorbing American events as its own and continuing its homage to freedom's tradition. The elusive soul of a city is certainly not to be grasped so easily, but the spiritual and intellectual history of Boston, and the founding of the United States of America, beckons one to walk this trail. As you read through this guide, give pause to the absolute beauty and significance of freedom, and deeply reflect upon those who first had the courage, the vision, the perseverance, and the grace to ensure such freedom. After all, America is—in so very many respects, and in its essence—the first child born of the Age of Reason.

Even though I walk the same path again and again, I shall never find the last blossom.

—Katherine Gladney Wells, *Psalm for Myself*

Just to breathe in a little space, calmness,
sunlight, and . . . history.

BOSTON'S COMMON GROUND

Looking over this lovely and impressive landscape, it is difficult to imagine the heavy presence of thousands of British Royal troops. In their imposing uniforms, swords and cannon at the ready, they trained from sunrise to sunset on this Common Ground and in clear view of Bostonians. King George III, under whose command they all pledged their allegiance, was steadfast in his determination and commitment to put an end to his colony's rebellious ways. Most patriots were intimidated and anxious with the presence of so many red coats, yet they intensely studied their oppressors' every move in preparation for the ensuing battles. Prior to the Common being a training ground, William Blackstone sold this land, once his pasture, to the Puritan townspeople, and since independence, these forty-four acres of land have remained a place where public demonstrations and jubilant celebrations have taken place. So many sit peacefully now—under great white clouds and surrounded by tall oaks, impressive monuments, and pretty fountains—as the soft wind blows through leaves. It is hoped one hears the distant whispers of those men and women who filled the streets and homes and gardens of Boston in the 1700s and who fought for and shaped this young country. It is hoped, too, that one hears the bold words of Reverend Martin Luther King Jr., as he held the flame of justice up to the darkness of segregation, in front of a crowd of twenty-two thousand, on this very land in April of 1965. Truly the setting of America's story of independence, the Boston Common is a place where words stand strong like the great oaks.

Each droplet, tokens of friendship and admiration.

THE BREWER FOUNTAIN

The truth and beauty of this fountain lie both in reality and in metaphor. Generously donated to the city of Boston by Gardner Brewer, a resident businessman and generous philanthropist, this fountain—magnificently crafted in Paris by French artist Michel Joseph Napoléon Liénard for the 1855 Paris World Fair—has come to symbolize the deep historical, philosophical, and political connection shared by France and America. The words of Thomas Paine and Benjamin Franklin, two leading men in the founding of the American Republic, echoed the ideas set forth from the Age of Enlightenment, specifically from French philosophers Denis Diderot and Voltaire. The allure of independence and self-governance, and the movement away from the corruption of the Christian Church in its efforts to acquire political power, were fundamental tenets of this new and critical political radicalism. This ornate and remarkable fountain is an endearing and enduring reminder that it was French philosophers who planted the seeds of America's discontent, and its quest for independence. It was France who first recognized the United States of America as a sovereign nation, and it was the French who provided weapons and loans along with an army and a navy to serve in concert with those under the command of George Washington. Fountains sing the song of the city in which they stand, and fountains refresh one's knowledge of the past while providing hope for the future. In its essence, the Brewer Fountain, standing pretty on the Boston Common across from the Park Street Church, exemplifies the deep roots shared with France, and the strength of America's spirit of independence.

The courage of those whose sheer resolve
prompts them to take on such a giant.

SHAW MONUMENT

The distinguished Shaw Monument by sculptor Augustus Saint-Gaudens—the first of its kind to depict and acknowledge the significant and selfless contribution made by African Americans during the Civil War—stands tall while facing, invitingly, toward Beacon Hill's Black Heritage Trail. To study the faces of those marching forward, to fight in perfect line, is to recognize the long shadow of racial divide that has blanketed America's past and haunts its present. Within the eyes of each bronze-cast face is the story of America, the story of suffering and perseverance, the story of hope and promise. These men of the 54th Massachusetts Regiment, determined to disprove the widespread belief that Negros were inferior and lacked the courage necessary to be soldiers, were willing to sacrifice their lives to preserve and to strengthen the ideals set forth by President Abraham Lincoln. Riding at attention atop a well-muscled horse, with the winged angel of victory and peace above, is Colonel Robert Gould Shaw, a Harvard-educated officer and the son of a prominent Boston abolitionist family who risked both reputation and life in order to lead the black soldiers of the 54th. On July 18, 1863, fighting alongside his men in South Carolina in the bloody assault on Fort Wagner where 272 of his troops fell dead, Shaw was killed, stripped of his uniform, and thrown by the Confederates into a mass grave. What was intended to be an insult was, according to Robert's parents, an honor, and precisely where their son would have wished to be buried—buried and surrounded by the brave and free men of the 54th.

See the breath, them breathing, and the look in their eyes . . .
who would not be moved by such a struggle.

BLACK HERITAGE TRAIL

"What to the slave is the fourth of July?" These poignant words were spoken by the distinguished African American abolitionist Frederick Douglass in 1852 at an Independence Day speech where he then went further, saying, "This fourth of July is yours, not mine. You may rejoice, I must mourn." When principle meets passion, noble and noteworthy feats are accomplished. The Black Heritage Trail, both heroic and humble in nature, embodies the resounding determination of black Americans to confront and defeat the injustices of slavery, oppression, and racism. This is a great path of strength and hope—one that begins beside the 54th Regiment Memorial and winds its way through Beacon Hill's fourteen pre–Civil War structures and historic sites—where the visitor is easily lost in contemplation and caught up in self-reflection. With the passing of the 13th Amendment to the Constitution in 1865, the United States abolished slavery. But it was in 1783, nearly a century earlier—and in great part due to the righteous perseverance of a slave named Quock Walker who sued for, and won his freedom—that the Massachusetts Supreme Court ruled in favor to end slavery. With this ruling, Beacon Hill's North Slope quickly became home to a free black neighborhood where community support, institutions, and education sang and danced with principle and passion, thereby providing the flickering light of freedom that was much needed throughout America. This path, one well worn by the dedicated and determined shoes of Frederick Douglass, and well traveled by slaves escaping along the Underground Railroad, represents the greatest sadness and the greatest gladness in America's storied history.

*Lights at night reflect memories while revealing
a whole world of new ideas.*

Massachusetts State House

Before this graceful and commanding State House was reconstructed in the year 1798, there were three hills that stood in the center of Boston. Two were leveled, the soil used to fill the surrounding water to extend Boston's buildable land, while one, Beacon Hill, was smoothed by fifty feet to make space for this new State House. The original State House on Washington Street had served the people and the principles of liberty well, but with the passage of time it did not seem grand or large enough to be representative of an enduring temple to democracy. Noted architect Charles Bulfinch designed this structure, and did so to exemplify and accentuate the permanency and the promise of a burgeoning self-governed country. The impressive and reflective golden gilded dome was not always such, as whitewashed wooden shingles were there originally, years before Paul Revere embellished freedom's dome in copper. During World War II, dark paint concealed the dome, protecting the State House and the unlit city surrounding it from the possibility of aerial attack. Various leaders, educators, and martyrs have been cast in stone and adorn the lawns of the State House; the latest, America's 35th President, John F. Kennedy, encompasses the spirit of America's optimism and its unyielding determination to move forward toward freedom's promise. In 1999, to recognize and honor the profound contributions of women to public life in Massachusetts, a lovely series titled *Hear Us* was permanently installed within the State House. It is as though every detail of this magnificent new State House—since its inception to present—casts a bright and lasting light on the struggle for, and ultimate triumph of, freedom.

The greater sounds of a modern city, silenced by the faded past of such a place.

PARK STREET CHURCH

With its poignant words, "Long may our land be bright/With freedom's holy light," the song *America*, also known as *My Country 'Tis Of Thee*, was sung publicly by Sunday school children for the first time on July 4, 1831, on the rounded stone steps that usher visitors into this significant and striking landmark. Once the tallest building in the city, architect Peter Banner, chief mason Benajah Young, and woodcarver Solomon Willard oversaw the building of this impressive church in the year 1809. Placing the 217-foot steeple atop in 1810 marked the beginning of the beautification of Boston, and before the waterways surrounding Boston were filled in, someone arriving by ship could see the church from all directions. Throughout the time of America's revolution against the British, this was the site of the town granary, and, during the War of 1812—again, with the British—gunpowder was discreetly hidden within the dark chambers of the church's basement. By 1829, Park Street Church mirrored the antislavery sentiment held by Bostonians, as twenty-three-year-old William Lloyd Garrison, Boston's leading abolitionist, delivered his enlightened address stating that black Americans should be freed, given an education, and accepted as equal citizens with whites. With nearly 1,500 people present, Garrison went on to state that there was no valid legal or religious justification for the preservation of slavery. This understated and yet elegant church helped America draw nearer to its destiny, its destiny as a beacon for all who wish to live in the sweet land of liberty.

These powerful and telling stones—
such aspirations, sufferings, and passions.

GRANARY BURYING GROUND

It takes but a light easterly sun to warm the headstones of this graveyard enough to ignite the distant flame of America's independence. This small square of tattered land mirrors the rough landscape of freedom that our forefathers encountered. Deep below the stones rest the remains of Samuel Adams, John Hancock, and Robert Treat Paine, three signers of America's Declaration of Independence. Immediately off to the right lay the five victims of the Boston Massacre—and a sixth, a twelve-year-old boy, Christopher Seider, who was the first to die in the political strife that later became the American Revolution and whose death heightened tensions that erupted into the Boston Massacre. To the left, James Otis, the patriot and lawyer to whom the phrase "Taxation without representation is tyranny" is often attributed, quietly rests. Still, further into the hallowed ground, one will encounter the graves of Paul Revere and Peter Faneuil, and the careful observer in search of a more whimsical figure may even discover an Elizabeth Goose—often referred to as "America's Mother Goose" by so many well-read children. Certainly the loudest of all stones within this radiant serenity is the Franklin Monument. Here rests Benjamin Franklin's parents, Josiah and Abiah, as Franklin, himself, is buried at the Christ Church Burial Ground in Philadelphia along with four other signers of the Declaration of Independence. Headstones may decay and crumble, but seeing winter's first snow faintly falling onto the headstones, and blanketing the sleep of so many of America's original patriots, or watching a summer sun slowly fade into a lilac evening, should stir the embers of admiration and awe for all who visit.

Certain churches serve beautifully, in their small solitude and
melancholy glow, to remind and awaken.

KING'S CHAPEL

Beauty can, at times, alarm the senses and ignite passions, and this particular church, on this corner and for a century, accomplished just that. In its classic Georgian structure with Greek-style columns, this church began as a small wooden chapel in 1687 and was erected as a message, a tyrannical gesture, from English colonial administrator Governor Andros. His message was simple and disquieting: Puritans, you may try to distance yourselves from England, the Crown, and the Anglican Church, but this I shall not allow. British authority appropriated this plot of land against the will of the Puritans. The chapel was built as the first Anglican Church in New England and was attended by Loyalists and, by 1753, the small wooden chapel—too plain and too tattered—was replaced by what is seen today. During the exile of Loyalists in 1776, however, and throughout the Revolution, patriots defiantly referred to the structure as the Stone Chapel. The lavish interior boasts having housed the very first church organ in New England, adorned, of course, with a gold crown. A bell, recast by Paul Revere in 1816 and said by Revere himself that "It is the sweetest bell I ever made," still rings every Sunday morning to summon parishioners to service. An elegant Gothic-revival wineglass pulpit, the oldest pulpit in America, completes the immaculate beauty of this chapel. Since its inception, lest one forgets, this structure stood boldly as a darkened symbol of religious and political control, and served to stir the embers of discontent, eventually igniting a revolution like no other.

e lyes Buried y̶

JOHN BECHA

o departed this

June the 17.th 177

Aged 77 Year

y the Man of Mortals ha

quiet Mind from Vain Des

neither Hopes deceive nor

ives at Peace within himf

ught or Act accountable

o his Confcience and his

Listen, and meet the ghosts of our earliest years,
then shout for the pleasure of being alive.

KING'S CHAPEL
BURYING GROUND

There is an intimate and reflective symphony of art, literature, and death that can be experienced within this, Boston's oldest, graveyard. The crooked rows of greenstone and slate seem to speak—through etchings of hourglasses, skulls, and crossed bones—as they whisper their brooding message concerning one's meager time on earth, and a life that is not meant to be fooled with, but lived fully. Poetic verse, carved in these headstones and always centering on the certainty of death, reminds the reader to repent, and embrace a life of virtue. Upon entering this burying ground, one encounters the intricately carved stone of Joseph Tapping, with its depiction of Father Time embroiled in an epic struggle with death, and the foretelling words "Time Flies. Remember That You Must Die." Looking closely, one will discover the resting place of Elizabeth Paine, thought to be Nathanial Hawthorne's inspiration for *The Scarlet Letter*, her gravestone forever inscribed, and ever branded, with the letter A in the minds of all who visit. In the center of all the great and common souls that rest within the black iron-speared gate of the King's Burying Ground, is the celebrated Mary Chilton, a passenger aboard the *Mayflower* in 1620 and the first European woman to step ashore at Plymouth Rock. Of all the whispers that float in the air of this graveyard, perhaps the most haunting and disconcerting come from those Puritans whose souls attempt to rest knowing that they are forever attached to King's Chapel, a chapel representing the Anglican church from which they fled, and one they viewed as being oppressive and corrupt.

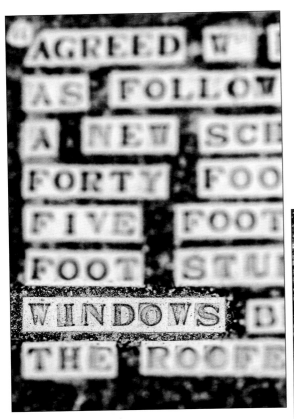

One must open a window, insistent in its truthfulness.

First Public School— Site of Boston Latin School

Gazing at the whimsical mosaic that signifies the place where the first public school building in America once stood is like looking through a window and into the past. For the first time in America, in April of 1635, children learned and played together under one roof with the watchful eye of Schole-Master Philemon Pormont and with the support of public funds. That said, however, parents during these early years were encouraged to assist in their child's education by providing firewood for the school. One always knew, by which child was furthest from the fireplace and left cold and shivering, whose parent was derelict in his responsibility. By the time of the Revolution, this school, known to all as Boston Grammar School, fostered a strong sense of responsible dissent in its children, strong enough, even, for British commanders to take note. Our forefathers believed that education—rooted within the souls and intellect of the children—would protect the essence of democracy and thereby safeguard the ideals of liberty. Five signers of America's hallowed Declaration of Independence attended this first public school, and, years later, as the school became known to all as Boston Latin School, Ralph Waldo Emerson, Leonard Bernstein, and Helen Magill White—the first woman to earn a PhD in the United States—would grace its doors. The purpose of public education is to turn mirrors into windows—to see beyond oneself—and this lovely and lasting ideal and sentiment began inside the small wooden building that once stood upon this mosaic.

So much influence, everywhere and always,
through his labor and his talent.

Benjamin Franklin Statue

America's first diplomat to be received by any foreign government, Benjamin Franklin returned from Paris to a newly constituted United States. He returned a hero after having secured financial and military support from France for America's independence. France, a country already embroiled in the many significant and progressive changes brought on by the Age of Enlightenment, not only wished to avenge their loss to Britain in the Seven Years' War but also recognized that an independent and free America would strengthen the ideals and philosophies held dear by its citizens. Throughout his life, Benjamin Franklin exemplified the spirit of American ingenuity and drive, as proven by his many inventions. The first volunteer fire company, the first insurance company, the first hospital, the printing press and lightning rod and bifocals and the glass harmonica, these we owe to the curious and active mind of a man who left school at the age of ten. Although his formal education ceased at an early age, Benjamin was an insatiable learner on his own and later in his life spoke out against traditional education and spoke in favor of a more student-led educational experience. "Tell me and I forget. Teach me and I remember. Involve me and I learn," was his educational refrain. Upon closer inspection, and perhaps equally as important to all accomplishments, this statue—Boston's first public portrait statue—attempts to capture both the inventive and philosophical likeness of Franklin as well as the less serious and more humorous side of this great patriot. One year after George Washington assumed the office of President of the United States, Benjamin Franklin—nicknamed "The First American" because of his unyielding campaign for colonial unity, and regarded as the best mind of the Founders—passed.

Unquestionably, they all nodded:
one must read, nothing but read.

OLD CORNER BOOKSTORE

A free and literate America was the ultimate wish of our founding fathers, and it is in this corner bookshop where all American literature has its roots. Newly released from the presses of Ticknor and Fields—Boston's iconic book publisher—Julia Howe's "Battle Hymn of the Republic" inspired America's deep sense of patriotism while the publication of Hawthorne's *The Scarlet Letter* scorched America's moral consciousness. Throughout time, and to date, literature has held the mirror up to America's identity, exposing its lovely features as well as its hideous blemishes. Clear and well-designed prose has always served to stir the individual mind and even move massive armies against tyranny. Being extraordinarily well read, our Founders coveted the words, ideals, and philosophies of Locke, Bayle, Hume, and Voltaire—those European minds that, early on, lit the flame of enlightenment. And it was within those philosophies where the birth of a new America, an America governed by reason and individualism rather than by tradition, arose and flourished. For well over one hundred years, this building housed *The Atlantic Monthly* whose founders, Emerson and Longfellow, wished to create a magazine dedicated to promoting writers and committed to expose and articulate the cultural and political issues that defined America. It is pleasing to think that this brick building has a voice of its own, a resilient voice that harks back to the 1600s when it was the home of Anne Hutchinson—a progressive and courageous advocate for civil liberty and America's first feminist theologian—and a voice that continues, no matter its occupancy, to inspire the pursuit of independence and of knowledge.

She shouts a message that is virtually incomprehensible, leaving visitors questioning all that they believe.

Boston Irish Famine Memorial

Known in all of Ireland as *An Drochshaol*, "The Bad Times," this darkly disquieting monument, sculpted by Robert Shure and commemorated in 1998, bears the heavy responsibility of symbolizing the horror and the misery of the worst humanitarian catastrophe to affect nineteenth century Europe: the Irish Famine. The pain of hunger—bodies curling into themselves like burning paper—led to one million deaths, while food, sowed in Irish soil by Irish hands, crossed the channel to pay English absentee landlords their rent. The agonizing lines taken from Amelia Blanford Edwards's poem, "Give Me Three Grains of Corn, Mother," continue to echo in the hearts of the Irish people, *What has poor Ireland done, Mother/What has poor Ireland done/That the world looks on, and sees us starve/Perishing one by one.* The people of Boston heard the melancholy cry of the Irish and responded in 1847 by sending the USS *Jamestown*, readied by a voluntary crew, from its Boston Harbor to Cork Harbor with 800 tons of provisions. Bostonians and Irish immigrants, immigrants whose ancestors helped fight in America's War for Independence, cast aside any differences for the greater good of humanity. The two juxtaposing statues—one depicting defeat and impending death, and the other portraying the hope for a better life for those who made the treacherous voyage to America in what were silently called Coffin Ships—convey the powerful and opposing emotions of this febrile period. Where history books have been vague, presenting the famine as merely a potato crop failure, this sculpture is clear and limitless in its power and in its unforgettable and haunting message.

One marvels at the inner world, still stirring with stories, of this modern city.

OLD SOUTH MEETING HOUSE

Under a gray sky, there is a vague sadness to this plain and simple building, yet under a bright sunlit day, its simplicity projects strength and promise. In 1669, this was a Puritan church made of cedar wood—simple in design, absent of ornament and elegance, and wholly focused on sermon over ceremonious drivel. By 1729, bricks replaced wood, and soon thereafter the fervent voices of notable patriotic orators such as John Hancock, Samuel Adams, and Dr. Joseph Warren echoed within. Crowds, so large in number that those speaking had to enter by ladder and through open windows, converged on this meeting place to vent their anger over British authority and rule. Of all the events leading up to America's War for Independence—most notably the Boston Massacre and the Boston Tea Party—this, the Old South Meeting House, is the sanctified ground in which the conviction needed for revolution flourished and sprung. There is a certain energy that stirs within and surrounds this ordinary yet inspiring building, an energy that is capable of moving individuals and even armies toward decisive and brilliant deeds. British soldiers, during the Siege of Boston in 1775, knew well that desecrating this Meeting House—by chopping its contents into firewood, and turning it into a horse stable and a bar—would pierce the psyche and disturb the souls of Bostonians, and they were spot on. Years after independence, Wendell Phillips, Boston's first mayor, boldly stated that the Old South Meeting House exemplifies "the memories of the most successful struggle the race has ever made for the liberties of man."

Where bold, essential, and stirring words
forever shed their light.

OLD STATE HOUSE

No other building in all of America reflects the power of the British Monarchy, and no other balcony in these United States echoes the control exerted by England over the colonists other than that of the Old State House. This State House was once seen as the great capital building of England's colony, and its western facing balcony was the place from which royal governors spoke their authoritative pronouncements to New Englanders dependent on the Crown. Beautifully set against a blue or gray sky, and bearing witness to a political sea change, the golden lion and unicorn that flank the balcony are the mighty symbols of the United Kingdom—the lion embodying England, and the unicorn, Scotland. Surrounded now by modern skyscrapers, this brick building holds within it the voluminous and progressive voice of James Otis, an esteemed lawyer. It was Otis who presented his eloquent argument against the Writ of Assistance in 1761, fifteen years before America's independence was declared. His was seen as a progressive and inspirational voice, alive with the flame of opposition and liberty. In 1776, as America's war for independence had commenced and the word "liberty" found lodgment in the hopes of Americans, this balcony supported Colonel Thomas Crafts as he stood tall and read, for the first time in Boston, the most influential of all political documents: the Declaration of Independence. And, later that evening, when stars dotted the night sky, a euphoric crowd celebrated on a grand scale by burning all symbols of royal authority, including, of course, the most noticeable and the most representative of the Crown, the lion and the unicorn.

Each visitor . . . her heart large enough to
accommodate the five.

Boston Massacre Site— Incident on King Street

On the cold evening of March 5, 1770, a peaceful blanket of winter's snow covered the cobblestones of Boston while a British soldier, private White, stood watch in his sentry box. Already, the temperature of discontent and rebellion throughout Boston was hot—boiling hot from the recent death of a twelve-year-old boy, Christopher Seider, who was killed, indiscriminately, while picketing against British imports. Out of the cold evening darkness came a shout of anger from an apprentice wigmaker to British officer John Goldfinch over an unpaid bill. As the private came to the defense of his officer, insults quickly cut the icy air and crowds of agitated Bostonians converged on the scene. British soldiers, with fixed bayonets, hastened to the growing mob in support of White and Goldfinch while church bells began ringing into the night. More people jammed the street and then more soldiers and then loud taunting and shouting and spitting and then objects flew through the air and angry eyes seared into scared eyes and then, in that chaotic and surreal moment—as if the winter air had momentarily frozen the scene—someone yelled, "Fire!" Three lay dead in the snow that night. Two others later died. Nine soldiers were tried, seven soldiers were acquitted, and two soldiers were found guilty of manslaughter. Their lawyer, the leading patriot John Adams, insisted that the jury see beyond the fact that the accused were Redcoats. Certainly, the events of this winter's night turned colonial sentiment further against King George III, laying a more determined foundation for revolution. But the lasting beauty is that of America's judicial system, a system reflected in the actions of John Adams on that cold night when he ensured that nine British soldiers would be guaranteed certain essential rights, including, and most importantly, unencumbered access to legal representation.

*A rebelliousness and resolve that now runs
dormant in the heart of every Bostonian.*

BOSTON TEA PARTY

Of all infusions, tea—so closely associated with the act of colonization, and forever linked to the American Revolution—possesses the least admirable reputation, as each dried leaf of the privileged is the product of the enslaved. And so it is no wonder why the inhabitants of Boston, still British citizens in 1773, strongly believed in the motto "no taxation without representation," and therefore rebelled against the Tea Act, an act meant to shore up Britain's failing East India Company. On the night of December 16, the Sons of Liberty, disguised as Mohawk Indians, stormed Griffin's Wharf, boarded three docked tea ships, and pitched the symbolic leaves—forty-six tons, enough to brew over eighteen-million cups—into Boston Harbor. This defiant act was, indeed, the match that lit the flame of war. When news of this treasonous act reached the ears of King George III, his eyes steeped with anger and he knew, with unabashed certainty, that New England was in need of a heavy hand. Quickly, the town of Boston turned crimson with Redcoats as its streets filled with British soldiers ready to subdue and control their heated and belligerent colony. Even with the king's harshly imposed penalties—such as the quartering of soldiers in privately owned homes and the banning of all political gatherings—the resilient and defiant people of Boston kept the spirit of independence within their sights. Not long after the troops returned, in April of 1775, the blood of the Patriots and the Redcoats would spill onto the fields of Lexington and Concord.

Listen . . . to the hushed voice of this old building:
the more I am threatened, the more courageous and striking I become.

FANEUIL HALL

There appears to linger, within the cobblestone promenade of Faneuil Hall, the memory of those whose voices and actions demanded, fought for, and won America's independence. Named after its founder, the wealthy bachelor and public benefactor Peter Faneuil, this was, and continues to be, Boston's lively and prosperous marketplace. The brick hall Mr. Faneuil had built on this space, and specifically its second-floor public meeting room, is what makes this an esteemed national landmark, one worthy of being known as The Cradle of Liberty. The defiant Samuel Adams and his protests against the Sugar and Stamp Acts, the brazen Dr. Joseph Warren and his rally against the Tea Tax, the secretive Sons of Liberty and their indignation over the Boston Massacre— all of these radical and revolutionary gatherings are what make this second-floor meeting room breathe with restlessness and upheaval, and seethe with the promise of liberty. A decade after the bloodshed ended and America's fight for independence was won, President George Washington visited Boston, atop a white horse, where he toured Harvard College, listened to a concert at the Stone Chapel, and attended an elegant dinner, as the guest of honor, at Faneuil Hall. Frederick Douglass's impassioned speech in 1849 addressing the stormy debate over colonizing people of color was delivered from within these walls, and Lucy Stone, the first woman from Massachusetts to earn a college degree and a fierce voice against slavery and for improving the rights of American women, chose Faneuil Hall in order to stir and support the issue of women's voting rights. It is here, throughout this vivacious marketplace—and within its great hall, where philosophical mindsets and unfaltering opposition are always welcome—that one's dreams may be easily taken for a walk.

"ILSE, A CHILDHOOD FRIEND of mine,
once found a raspberry in the camp
and carried it in her pocket all day
to present to me that night on a leaf.

IMAGINE A WORLD in which
your entire possession is
one raspberry and
you give it to your friend."

This etched glass is most discreet,
speaking slowly and in a low voice.

New England Holocaust Memorial

No one sense is left untouched by walking through these five glass pillars, as the annihilation of six million human beings is deafening. To read the words inscribed in stone paints a haunting image in the mind's eye, while the scent of steamed heat, slowly emerging from red embers, drifts up though metal grates to remind one of the ovens. This is a living memorial to those who were murdered in World War II, and this is a reminder to those who stood by, watched, and did nothing. Study World War I and the Treaty of Versailles; study the German economy in the 1920s and '30s; study the rise of Fascism; study the Spanish Civil War and the Night of Broken Glass and the fall of Poland and the Yellow Star of David . . . study all there is and, still, this memorial remains incomprehensible. But sit for a while. Sit and watch as people slowly walk and point to inscriptions, recoiling in disbelief. What is to be comprehended is the individual. Connect with just one life of the six million, and watch as she is shamed into wearing the star. Watch as she is loaded onto the train with armed guards shouting over the snarling barks of dogs. Watch as she gasps for air and longs for water in the hot car of the train. And when the door finally swings aside, watch her fall to the ground only to be pushed in line and marched into the death camp. See what she cannot believe she sees, and feel her shaking. There are very few places one can visit where lips fall silent as the mind screams.

Out there, contained within this city await an abundance
of flavors, events, speeches, dramas, and characters.

THE NORTH END

The place within Boston that has always embodied and embraced the spirit of independence and immigration is the North End. One quickly hears the faint whispers of freedom fade behind lively and authentic Italian voices, as this has been, since the beginning of the twentieth century, the home of Italian immigration. For the misty image of colonial Boston to present itself, imagine the North End of the 1700s as an island, one where two wooden drawbridges spanned Mill Creek to join it to the mainland. The innovative and patriotic spirit of Paul Revere undoubtedly fills the senses, as his unyielding quest for liberty drifts prominently throughout time. As a neighborhood where Boston's elite lived alongside artisans and laborers, although there were acts of violence committed throughout Boston both by Patriots and Redcoats, the North End was frequently targeted by Tories loyal to the crown and by British soldiers who, in one instance, tore down a meeting house for use as firewood. With America's independence underway, the North End, in the 1800s, became the heart of Irish immigration. Irish families who wished for better lives—free from the constraints of poverty and far from the pains of famine—found their home within these narrow streets and, through perseverance and with dignity, soon prospered and assimilated into Boston's mainland. Today, and for over one hundred years, generations of Italians have developed the North End into a welcoming and charming neighborhood environment. The present day, in this convivial place that many now refer to as "Boston's Kitchen," gives rise to possibilities while its past gives pause for contemplation.

Good to breathe in the timeless smell of timber,
and pause at the sturdy grace of this worn
painted wood.

PAUL REVERE HOUSE

When it rains, streaks of history—those captivating stories of its legendary occupant, Paul Revere—seem to run down the clapboards of this small, wooden house. One such story that began within the walls of this, Boston's oldest wooden building, is celebrated and immortalized by Henry Wadsworth Longfellow in his famous poem, *Paul Revere's Ride*—a poem that captures the exhilaration and vitality of Revere's ride to warn Samuel Adams, John Hancock, and the town militias that the Redcoats, seven-hundred strong, were on the attack. Five years prior to his epic ride, in 1770, Revere purchased this home in Boston's North Square where his first wife, their five children, his mother, and his patriotic ideals and revolutionary actions filled its seven rooms. As an activist and a messenger for the Sons of Liberty, and as an official currier for the Massachusetts Provincial Assembly to Congress, Revere set out from his home on multiple prior rides, including one to announce the arrival of British tea ships in Boston's harbor and another to report the celebrated news of the Boston Tea Party. Revere's home flourished with ideas for the first Continental currency and designs for the official seal of Massachusetts, and after America's independence was secured, Revere's entrepreneurial spirit turned to copper. The very copper that covers the State House dome, fittings still to be found aboard the USS *Constitution*, and simple and beautiful dinnerware, are all attributed to Revere's foundry. It seems that the harder the rain falls and cascades down the facade of this, Paul Revere's home, the louder the stories become.

Effortlessly holding the light of freedom in its walls until dusk, when a flame flickers into dark nights.

OLD NORTH CHURCH

To stop and stare in silence, up high to the steeple of Old North Church, and on a night when the moonlight is sharp and white, is to imagine the signal lanterns of Paul Revere being lit, one if by land, and, as it was, two if by water. Through this image, the essence of defiance and of determination on the very eve of America's Revolution, the eighteenth of April, in 1775, flows over all. What makes the lighting of the lanterns by Sexton Robert Newman in Old North most sardonic are its eight bells, cast in England in 1744, with one bearing the Crown's boisterous inscription, "We are the first ring of bells cast for the British Empire in North America." Built in 1723 as England's second Anglican Church in Boston and built perfectly to allow for streams of sunlight to pass through its many windows, prayers for the king eventually fell silent in support of rebellion. Underneath the church, in crypts, dark and decaying, are the graves of over one thousand bodies, including British soldiers, patriots of the Continental army, and children who had died of disease. By 1815, with the bright light of independence filling the spirits and guiding the actions of a new America, a bust of George Washington—the very first created to honor his presidency—was donated to the church for all to appreciate. American novelist Edith Wharton once wrote that, "There are two ways of spreading light: to be the candle or the mirror that reflects it." Old North is, indeed, the candle, and those who visit and reflect are, indeed, the mirrors.

*To stand in the midst of the most beautiful
and yet sorrowful landscape of life.*

COPP'S HILL
BURYING GROUND

When looked over fleetingly, the ambiance within this burying place conveys the charm of a certain kind of ugliness, its weathered stones seemingly characterizing a place of forgotten names and forgotten deeds. But when looked upon closely, the people, and their honest and good life led, surface and sing. Surrounded by a chorus of over a thousand slaves that rest here, the spirit of Prince Hall—an African American man with a powerful voice who railed against slavery and rallied for equal rights, especially the rights for black children to receive an education—sings out fearlessly within this burying ground. Robert Newman—the brave and selfless patriot who hung the warning lanterns up high in the Old North Church steeple so that patriots in Charlestown were able to see the two lights and spread the message that the Redcoats were attacking by water—silently, as if suspended forever in that one dark and decisive night, sings his song. And George Worthylake—the keeper of America's first lighthouse, Boston Light on Little Brewster Island, and the first to die in the line of duty—sings his song, a soft and lonely melody that seemingly illuminates all souls who rest within this graveyard. Mostly, within this much overlooked burying ground, are the bodies of ordinary people, good and common people whose lives were not touched by fame but, instead, were defined by that hard work where difficult days slowly turn into years. The songs they sing summon a spirit that simply will not break.

Contemplate the magnificence of its past and its enduring physical beauty.

USS *CONSTITUTION*
"OLD IRONSIDES"

This ship, whose proud decks seem to read like heroic novels and whose sails may be seen as unfinished pages to its glorious autobiography, has symbolized America's powerful and majestic presence upon the sea for over two centuries. As the ship that informed the light and the shade of liberty, she has circled the world, with exotic port calls in Zanzibar, Singapore, Cochinchina, Manila, Honolulu, and Rio de Janeiro, and she has fought gallantly for America's independence and for its right to conduct commerce, unobstructed, by way of sea. Named by President George Washington after the Constitution of the United States of America, this remains the oldest commissioned naval vessel afloat, and she has instilled both wonder and fear in the eyes, and throughout the souls, of her enemies. In the War of 1812, again a war with the British Empire, the *Constitution* earned her nickname, "Old Ironsides." It was off the coast of Nova Scotia—in one of the first of her thirty-three victorious battles—that the crew of the *Constitution* spotted a large sail on the horizon, a sail belonging to Her Majesty's Ship, the *Guerriere*. Eighteen-pound cannon balls, like meteors hurling through the ocean's air, slammed into the *Constitution*'s oak hull, only to appear to bounce off, falling harmlessly to the bottom of the sea. One sailor cried out in wonder and delight, "Huzza! Her sides are made of iron!" Now, fashioned slowly by the centuries, and radiant in her serenity, the USS *Constitution* is—as Oliver Wendell Holmes penned in his elegant and sentimental poem to her—the "ship in which the eyes of many visitors have danced to see."

These stones, set against the silence of the sky,
speak to the challenge that was hurled at an empire.

BUNKER HILL

Surrounded by so many streets and squares, so many gardens, houses, roofs, and chimneys, and overwhelming in its simple beauty and sturdy grace, the Bunker Hill Monument stands as a bold reminder that defending the principles of liberty, in victory or in defeat, is worth the fight. Rising into the depths of a Boston skyline, these granite stones mark the place where, on June 17, 1775—although untested, ill-equipped, and vastly outnumbered—the militia fought for the very first time as the newly established Continental Army against the British Army. In an effort to ensure that each shot fired met its mark, as the British began their charge, many believe it was Colonel William Prescott who spoke the infamous words to his regiment of patriots, "Do not fire until you see the whites of their eyes!" Although the British won this battle, yet suffered heavier losses, their victory instilled within them a sense of admiration for their enemy and uncertainty in their cause. As for the Americans, their defeat ushered in a strong wind of confidence throughout the thirteen colonies and an unwavering belief that the cost of independence was well worth dying for. Fifty years after the battle of Bunker Hill, on June 17, 1825, the Marquis de Lafayette—the French military officer, and confidant of George Washington, Alexander Hamilton, and Thomas Jefferson, who fought valiantly in America's War for Independence—returned to Boston to honor the battle itself and to lay the cornerstone to what is now the Bunker Hill Monument. At the proceeding banquet, one overflowing with thousands of people and good cheer, Lafayette raised his glass in admiration of America's holy resistance to oppression, and to the most beautiful patriotic fête ever celebrated.

Voices, continuing to echo, sizzle with rage
and drip with magnificence.

OTHER VOICES

Certainly there were voices that stood on center stage, and history has rewarded them with the gift of eternal recognition, but what of the other voices that comprised the chorus to America's independence? Lest we forget, here are but a few of the many voices, perhaps thousands, that are less known but equally significant:

"The waves have rolled upon me, the billows are repeatedly broken over me, yet I am not sunk down."

—MERCY OTIS WARREN (1728–1814)

Having the sound belief that women and men were of equal value in both mind and spirit, this influential writer was the first woman to have authored, in 1805, a three-volume history of the American Revolution.

"I desire you would remember the ladies . . . if we mean to have heroes, statesmen, and philosophers, we should have learned women."

—ABIGAIL ADAMS (1744–1818)

Suggesting to her husband, John Adams, that with the drafting of the Declaration of Independence, and with the creation of new laws, came the opportunity to make women equal to that of men, she passionately supported independence for all.

"Let me! I can ride as well as any man."

—SYBIL LUDINGTON (1761–1839)

At the young age of sixteen, with conviction and courage, she rode throughout the night, and more than twice the distance of Revere's ride, to alert the militia to the approaching threat of British forces.

"Has the God that made the white man and the black left any record declaring us a different species . . . are we not sustained by the same power, supported by the same food, and should we not then enjoy the same liberty."

—JAMES FORTEN (1766–1842)

Born a free black man, and after having served at a young age in the Continental Navy during the Revolution where his ship was captured and prisoner conditions poor, he continued, throughout his life, his quest for fairness and liberty for all.

"Now I can say loudly and openly what I have been saying to myself on my knees."

—DUKE ELLINGTON [ON] BARZILLAI LEW (1743–1822)

One of over one hundred African American soldiers who fought at the Battle of Bunker Hill, his talent as a fifer helped keep morale high with his version of "Yankee Doodle Dandy," and later, it was the Duke Ellington Orchestra that immortalized this patriot with a stirring piece dedicated in his honor.

*"Hazardous indeed were the offices [I] was appointed to perform . . .
having many times, at the peril of [my] own life entered the British
Camp and conveyed [back] to [my] General [Marquis de Lafayette] such
information as was deemed highly beneficial to the American cause."*

—JAMES ARMISTEAD LAFAYETTE (1748–1830)

An African American who served with distinction as a double agent for the
Continental Army, and whose intelligence gathering escapades helped allow
American forces to prevail at the Battle of Yorktown, this patriot successfully
petitioned for his freedom in 1787.

CULINARY

Virginia Woolf once remarked, "One cannot think well, love well, sleep well, if one has not dined well." Along Boston's Freedom Trail, as one walks out of the twenty-first century and into the eighteenth, there emerges a symphony of restaurants, bars, cafés, and taverns from which to choose. The elegant Omni Parker House—America's longest continually operating hotel, located across from King's Chapel and King's Chapel Burying Ground—invented and perfected the official state dessert of Massachusetts, the Boston Cream Pie. This historic treat seems to pair beautifully with any good bourbon Manhattan made in The Last Hurrah, the Parker House's famed whiskey bar. Tucked behind the statue of Benjamin Franklin is the stately Ruth's Chris Steak House where a memorable meal in a beautifully renovated historic setting may be experienced. Just near Faneuil Hall, on Union Street, are two taverns—the Bell In Hand and the Union Oyster House—each possessing the spirit of independence, each convivial beyond one's imagination, and each offering an endless tap of Samuel Adams Boston Lager. Walking down Hanover Street, and across the lovely and relaxing North End parks, is the North End, with its charming ambiance and where the freshest regional ingredients seem to linger in the breeze. Perhaps the best pizza in all the world—along with the most charismatic waitstaff—Regina's, on Thacher Street, beckons a visit. For a more formal Italian experience, Restorante Villa Francesca, on Richmond Street—a restaurant seemingly chasing perfection—peacefully awaits. Boston's Freedom Trail is a historic and a culinary journey, both filled with interest and intrigue, both designed for sharing, and both to be fully embraced.

OVERNIGHT

The simplicity and charm of a hotel room—especially after walking while admiring the wonders of the Freedom Trail—is always alluring and may be experienced on many affordable and handsome levels within the city of Boston. Situated neatly along School Street and directly alongside the Trail is the Omni Parker House, a profoundly historic hotel that first opened its doors in 1855 and welcomed guests such as literary greats Ralph Waldo Emerson and Henry David Thoreau, iconic athletes Babe Ruth and Ted Williams, and esteemed politicians Franklin Delano Roosevelt and John F. Kennedy. The Parker House boasts a Freedom Trail Family Suite, complete with a large-scale mural displaying the route and landmarks of the Trail. If a view of the luxurious Public Garden sounds inspiring, the first botanical garden in America, the splendid Four Seasons Hotel located at 200 Boylston Street is the worthy choice. At night from one of its freshly renovated rooms up high, one can gaze upon the illuminated golden dome of the State House, perhaps while sipping from a tall crystal flute of Perrier Jouët Belle Epoque. And for those travelers who wish for the charm and intimacy of a peaceful boutique hotel, there at 25 Charles Street, nearby the magnificent Boston Common, sits the Beacon Hill Hotel & Bistro. The twelve guestrooms and one suite that comprise this delightful hotel are quintessentially Boston, and the top floor terrace, with its flowered décor, offers a relaxing place from which to contemplate one's visit. Now, with three notable options offering three unique experiences, the celebrated City of Boston and its Freedom Trail patiently and invitingly await.

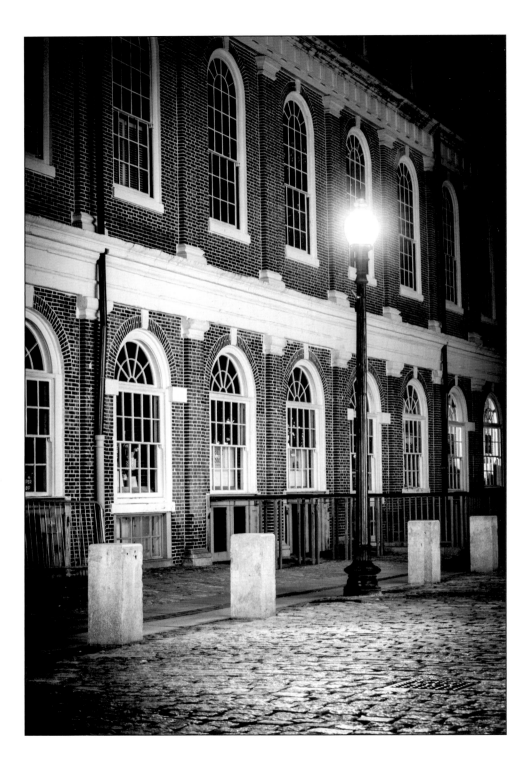

THE END

This is a time of pure astonishment,
grazing the edge of all significance,
brighter for one swift blinding moment than
the fires of all corruptions, tears, and wars;
so complex in its clean simplicity
that nothing need be offered in response.
—KATHERINE GLADNEY WELLS, *THE LONG WAIT*

ACKNOWLEDGMENTS

A warm appreciation to Anna Solo, a gifted photographer and now a good friend; to Amy Palmer, a talented artist and the closest of friends; to Keith Walsh, whose honest and sentimental reflections on his Ireland inspired the Irish Famine Memorial paragraph; to Jim Koch and Sally Jackson of The Boston Beer Company (cheers to Samuel Adams); to Dan McCole, a brilliant and significant painter whom I am privileged to know; and to the vibrant and generous Suzanne Shultz, CEO of Canvas Fine Arts in Boston. Grateful always to my wife, Meme, my parents, Robert and Gloria, and my mother- and father-in-law, Douglas and Katie. Thank you, as well, to the inspiring poet, the late Katherine Gladney Wells—mother to Katie, grandmother to Meme, and GG to Emma and Helen; the lovely friends and considerate editors, John and Marsha Robinson; and the publishing team at Skyhorse Publishing, especially Bill Wolfsthal and Leah Zarra. To Suzanne Taylor and to Sam Jones, and to the entire Freedom Trail Foundation, I appreciate your assistance, support, and endorsement. Always in my corner, and the best literary agency I could hope for, thank you to Peter and Sandra Riva of International Transactions.

OPPOSITE PAGE: *Designed by Amy Palmer*

ROBERT WHEELER

First pushing a stroller, then walking hand-in-hand, Robert recalls fondly the time spent with his two daughters along Boston's Freedom Trail. The rich and fascinating stories evoked by each historic site, as well as the exceptional charm of Boston's quaint city streets, shops, and restaurants were enough to lure Robert over and again for years and to inspire this sensory and absorbing book. Robert is the author of *Hemingway's Paris: A Writer's City in Words and Images* and *Hemingway's Havana: A Reflection of the Writer's Life in Cuba.* He lives in New Castle, New Hampshire, near the sea with his wife, Meme, while daughters, Emma and Helen, now grown, live in Boston and New York City.

ANNA SOLO

Anna is a photojournalist and documentary storyteller. Though she grew up in New York City, she developed a love for New England from a young age, leading to a move to Portsmouth, New Hampshire, where she now resides. Her work with both local and national publications keeps her traveling back to New York, but collaborating on this book about Boston has allowed her to expand the bounds of her photography. Immersing herself in the history of the Freedom Trail, while appreciating its place in a modern city, has led to images that allow the viewer to see into the past while being connected to the present. She enjoys all four New England seasons with her husband, Kenneth, and dog, Brooklyn.